BRIAN CARDINAL

Citizen Pain

by
Fred Kroner

SPORTS PUBLISHING LLC
www.SportsPublishingLLC.com

Director of production:
    Susan M. Moyer
Cover design:
    Christina Cary
Photos:
    Tom Campbell,
    *Gold and Black
    Illustrated*
Detroit photos:
    Allen Einstein,
    Einstein Photos

ISBN: 1-58261-451-2

SPORTS PUBLISHING LLC
www.SportsPublishingLLC.com

Printed in the United States.

*(Photo courtesy of Gold and Black
Illustrated)*

For Devin
No father could be more proud of a son

———————————————

Acknowledgments

Rod and Mary Cardinal, for not only sharing their memories and opinions, but also their vast assortment of scrapbooks.

My wife, Emily, for her diligence in proofreading and editing.

My son, Devin, for sharing his expertise on NBA players and roster moves.

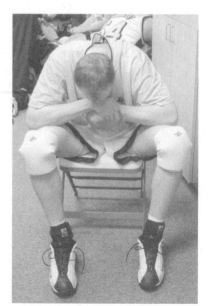

Walter J. Pierce and Sports Publishing, for allowing me to join the list of published authors.

Brian Cardinal, for being instrumental in contacting many of the persons who were interviewed for this book.

Don Akers, for researching Cardinal's complete high school statistics.

Thank you.

(Photo courtesy of Gold and Black Illustrated)

Contents

Brian is always willing to sign autographs. *(Photo courtesy of Brian Cardinal)*

CHAPTER ONE

in the Beginning

O ur story officially starts in the early morning hours of May 2, 1977. It was a Monday.

The second of Mary and Rod Cardinal's three children was born. Brian Lee Cardinal was 10 pounds, 7 ounces at birth and almost 22 inches long.

Perhaps his large size at birth was a foreshadowing of the big things that were to come in his athletic career.

By the time Brian was in grade school, he was starting to become aware of his dream.

"Growing up and being around Illinois basketball, I always wanted to do what they did," Brian said.

"I always wanted to sign autographs and to someday walk in the mall and have someone walking the other way say, 'Hey, there's Brian Cardinal,' like people did when I was walking around with [ex-Illini] Nick Anderson.

"They'd say, 'Hey, it's Nick Anderson. Can I get your autograph?' I know it sounds cheesy, but it's something I wanted. I knew the only way to achieve that dream is through hard work and dedication and setting goals for yourself."

Cardinal himself was something of an autograph hound in his formative years.

"Nick Anderson was my idol," he said. "Every picture that was in The *Champaign-Urbana News-Gazette*, I cut out and had him sign. I had 50 million pictures autographed."

In many respects, Brian Cardinal was like thousands— maybe millions—of children. They grow up in a small town and play sports as something to do. They all have heroes, and they all seek to be the ones who make something of themselves playing a game.

Some make their high school varsity team. The really good ones—less than one percent, according to 1999 statistics—go on to play in college. A few elite athletes wind up playing the game professionally.

***Brian in California at the Rose Bowl with the Fighting Illini
football team.*** *(Photo courtesy of Brian Cardinal)*

Brian Cardinal is one of the fortunate ones. He has
made the rounds.

"Anybody from a small town might pinch themselves
and say, 'That's one of us out there,' " said Gary Wilsey, an
assistant coach at Unity High School during Cardinal's career.

"They felt he represented small-town basketball. That's why it's fun to root for him."

Marty Blake, 74, the director of scouting for the NBA, can relate to that feeling.

"He should be an inspiration to anybody," Blake said. "He comes to play every day. I like Cardinal."

So, too, does Keith Glass, Cardinal's former agent.

"He could be anybody," Glass said. "What makes him marketable is that everybody who goes to a game can relate to him. He's not 7-foot or 6-10 and athletically gifted."

Inspired by a dream and a commitment to work for it, Brian made himself into a high school superstar, a player regarded as one of the top 100 prep seniors in the United States before he graduated in 1995 from Tolono's Unity High School.

He went on to Purdue University, in West Lafayette, Indiana, where he became one of that school's all-time basketball greats before earning his degree in business management in 2000.

In the NBA's 2000 draft, Cardinal was a second-round choice of the Detroit Pistons. The 6-8 forward made the team and earned almost $317,000 as a rookie.

"There's no way on earth if I could have mapped out at a young age how I wanted things to work out, that I would have mapped this out," Brian said. "Just to get where I'm at now is truly amazing."

Is it, or is this what dreams are all about?

Brian Cardinal can answer that question.

"Most normal people fall asleep and dream, and when they wake, they remember their dream briefly," Brian said. "I tell people I wake to my dream every day.

"My dream is reality."

And this is his story.

Brian's first point in the NBA was a free throw. (Photo courtesy of Einstein Photos)

CHAPTER TWO

Words of Wisdom

Everyone remembers comments his parents repeated that are memorable.

Brian Cardinal is no exception.

"I was brought up that hard work pays off, hard work is what takes you places; it's what helps dreams come true," Brian said.

"With that idea instilled in me, I took it and ran with it with basketball."

From the days the Cardinals took summer family vacations to visit relatives in Minnesota, Brian knew where he wanted to go.

"I recall a van ride," his older brother Troy said, "talking about what we wanted to be. I was in seventh or eighth grade, and Brian [who was in fifth or sixth grade] asked, 'Do you think I could ever play in the Big Ten?'

"Dad said, 'You can do whatever you want to do.' "

Brian Cardinal's path was set.

He was a ball boy at the University of Illinois during one of the glory years for the Illini, when the 1989 team went to the Final Four. His unique, behind-the-scenes view was not available to everyone, and he cherished it.

"I think it was a huge part of the development, to see the commitment that was made on

Brian in sixth grade in 1988. (Photo courtesy of Brian Cardinal)

the players' part, the Nick Andersons, the Kendall Gills, the Kenny Normans— just to see how much work they put into it," said Rod Cardinal. "People are used to seeing the games—that's what everybody sees and identifies with— but they were able to see what was involved with the travel, the practice, and preparation, and realized if you are going to make that kind of commitment, it's a big investment."

If he wasn't playing basketball in his driveway or at school, Brian Cardinal was watching others play at the U of I.

Each area had its rewards.

"It had a huge impact, to see all those great players," Brian said. "My brother and I would get to the gym a half-hour before Dad was supposed to be there and mess around on the court, rebounding for guys and passing balls.

"To watch the time they put into this dream they had of being great, I truly believe [it] played a huge role in how I evolved as a player and who I am today."

Mary Cardinal looked forward to the days her husband would take an afternoon break and come home. For her, it meant a break as well.

Her husband, Rod, is a trainer at the University of Illinois, where he has worked for 28 years. He tends to the injuries and ailments of the athletes—especially in men's basketball—at the Big Ten Conference school.

His quick trips home meant more than a chance to visit.

"A lot of time, Rod took the boys to practices, just to get them out of the house," Mary Cardinal said.

Brian and Troy with Harlem Globetrotter Sweet Lou Dunbar. *(Photo courtesy of Brian Cardinal)*

"They were both a handful," she said. "I don't know if it was because they competed a lot with each other, or just because they are two boys two years apart.

"Neither of them were angels. If they were, they probably wouldn't be the kind of people they are today."

It was not difficult for Rod Cardinal to get his sons after school or let them accompany him on weekends. The distance from the family home in east Tolono to the practice site at the University of Illinois Assembly Hall in Champaign was less than nine miles.

"Brian was an active kid and needed some way to channel his energy," Rod said. "Athletics was something that fit right in with keeping him busy, particularly as he would tag along up here.

"When there would be things I needed to get done in the office, he'd be able to entertain himself, either throwing a ball in Memorial Stadium or shooting baskets while we were in camp."

The Cardinals were growing up during an era when universities didn't face as many rules and restrictions by which they are now governed.

"That was before we were limited to 20 hours per week [to practice]," Rod Cardinal said. "We could go seven days a week. We always had practices and shootarounds."

As youngsters, the Cardinal children had no favorites between baseball, basketball, and football. Whichever sport was in season was the one they played.

"When Brian played baseball, we had the coaches make him a catcher," Rod Cardinal said. "Then [he would be] the center of activity on virtually every play rather than having him stuck in the infield or outfield where he had time to daydream.

"He was always better if you kept him involved and kept him busy."

Former teammate Joe O'Neill has a favorite memory from their Little League career.

"One time in the sixth inning, he came to the mound like something was wrong," O'Neill said. "So we asked, 'What do you want to do with this batter?'

"He was like, 'I don't know, I just needed a break.' He was always cracking jokes. I remember in tough games, Brian would talk to the batters and make them laugh."

As Brian grew older, however, his jovial nature occasionally took a back seat. He did not always welcome the feedback he received from his dad on the way home from basketball games.

When Rod Cardinal got the feeling his younger son was no longer listening to his words, he found a creative way to get him a message.

"When it got to the point we couldn't make adjustments on anything, we resorted to writing notes," Rod Cardinal said. "Things like, 'Work harder with your left hand. Turn the other way. Keep your head up.' Things he had probably heard from Coach Don Akers a million times and probably didn't want to hear from Dad."

Rod Cardinal has reason to believe the notes served their purpose. "After a while, we found where they stashed a bunch of them and would refer to them in different situations," he said.

Brian, sister Lisa, Troy's wife Betsy, Troy, Brian's mother Mary, and his father Rod at Troy and Betsy's wedding. *(Photo courtesy of Brian Cardinal)*

CHAPTER THREE

Two Boys, One Game

Kevin Costner, he was not.

Brian Cardinal is not an actor, but nonetheless shares a strong characteristic with one of the roles played by the Hollywood star.

Costner's character in *For Love of the Game*, Billy Chapel, was a baseball pitcher for the Detroit Tigers. Cardinal shares Chapel's passion, except his sport of choice is basketball.

Cardinal wasn't always a natural for the game.

"When I was younger, people made fun of me because I had a little push shot," Brian said. "I shot the ball with two hands. People said I shot like a grandma."

By the time he became a high school freshman, Cardinal had put other sports aside. Basketball alone was his focus.

"I figured if I was going anywhere, whether it was Parkland, Illinois, or wherever—with any sport, it was going to be basketball," he said. "That's when I started playing basketball year round."

His friends took notice.

"You'd always see Brian in the gym," said Joe O'Neill, who graduated from Unity High School in 1994. "He never stopped thinking about basketball and how he could get better."

Eric Stevens graduated from Unity the same year as Cardinal (1995). He said Brian elevated his game quicker than his teammates.

"It seemed like the only thing we did was play ball," said Stevens, who watched Cardinal blossom as a player.

"It felt good to know Brian was the buzz going into high school. He'd jumped a couple years ahead of us. We worked hard to be able to play with him."

Basketball was a bond for the Cardinal boys, though their relationship was often more antagonistic than friendly.

Brian with Unity teammate Eric Stevens. *(Photo courtesy of Brian Cardinal)*

"We didn't get along too well," Troy Cardinal said. "It was a typical older brother-younger brother type thing. We didn't see eye to eye."

When it became obvious that Brian was going to meet his lone preseason goal as a high school freshman ("I wanted to dress varsity," he said,) the brothers realized that for the sake of team harmony, they couldn't continue their family feud.

Rod Cardinal helped the boys come to terms with their sibling rivalry.

"With Brian and me being so incredibly competitive, it would have been easy to have had a rivalry," Troy Cardinal said. "As the season played out, I sat down and talked to my father.

"He said the two things that are most important are family and basketball. Family is most important, and we had to realize the rest of our lives we'd be related.

"Once we started realizing that, and that winning was the ultimate goal in basketball, it was easy to put away the competitiveness or trying to one-up the other."

Their two years as starters for Unity's varsity team helped nurture a lasting friendship. By the time Troy graduated in 1993—after Brian's sophomore year—he knew he had a special friend.

"From my senior year on, without a doubt, I knew he would be the best man in my wedding," Troy Cardinal said.

Brian Cardinal not only fulfilled that expectation in October 2000, but also "was the guy who gave me the most unbelievable toast at my wedding [to Betsy Skinner]," Troy said.

C H A P T E R   F O U R

Becoming a Gym Rat

Don Akers had coached Unity High School basketball teams the previous decade but stepped aside as he climbed the ladder in administration.

Now the principal at the school, Akers returned to the sidelines for the 1990-91 school year. He was aware that Brian Cardinal was an up-and-coming prospect, but he didn't know what to expect.

"I'd never coached a kid of that quality," Akers said. "I wasn't sure how far he could develop.

"As a freshman, he saw and did things some of the older players didn't do. He had a great sense for the game."

The following four years would be filled with game-winning shots, standout defensive plays, and important rebounds. What Akers remembers most, however, were times when Brian wasn't wearing his game jersey.

"He took his natural talent and worked and worked and worked," Akers said. "He and C.J. Franks [1997 Unity graduate] probably spent more hours in the gym than I've seen in this program.

"Brian was better than any of them, but he also out-worked any kid who played for me. His best games were our big games. The kid was always mentally tough."

Franks' father, Larry, can vouch for how many hours Cardinal dedicated to basketball during his high school years.

"They'd start playing [in the driveway] at 7:30 p.m., and I'd have to go out at 3 a.m. and get them to stop," Larry Franks said. "From an early age, the thing that impressed me was how hard he worked. His work ethic carried over to C.J. and they fed off of each other."

Cardinal's legacy (besides the No. 35 uniform in the school's trophy case) is his unfaltering commitment.

"He'd come home from a date, and it would be midnight and he'd go out in the driveway and shoot for a half-

Brian at the ceremony retiring his high school jersey. (Photo courtesy of Brian Cardinal)

hour or hour under the street lights," said his father, Rod Cardinal. "There'd be nights Brian didn't have anything to do, and he'd call up Coach [Gary] Wilsey at 11 o'clock, and they'd go meet at the high school and shoot around for a while. His energy level and activity level was certainly at a higher level than others."

Brian Cardinal made sacrifices, and he appreciates the efforts made by others on his behalf.

"A lot of credit goes to Coach Wilsey and to Coach Akers for spending time with me in the gym," Brian said. "Even after games, I'd go in there and shoot, because I was mad I didn't play well or shoot well.

"The bus would drop us off [after a road trip], and everybody would take off. Either Coach Akers or Coach Wilsey would stay behind and let me shoot.

"A lot of my friends would go out partying on Friday or Saturday nights. Coach Wilsey and I would be shooting or dribbling or doing different things with the basketball."

Rod Cardinal said, "It was easy for him, while things were fresh in his mind, to go back in the gym."

Brian Cardinal's dedication was not limited to late at night.

"He shot every morning before school, almost year round," Akers said. "He'd be in the gym when I got there [for practice], and he shot after practice and at open gyms when we had them on Wednesdays and Sundays during the season.

"I've never had a kid shoot any more than he did. Between his sophomore and junior years, he must have shot thousands of 'threes' to have that in his weaponry."

Larry Franks, who coached Cardinal on summer-league teams, saw in his star player a willingness to work on more than areas where he excelled.

"The good things he did, he didn't concentrate on them as much," Franks said. "The summer before his junior year [in high school], he shot threes, and it was unbelievable how much more range he had. Then, his ball-handling skills came along."

Cardinal recognized at an early age that to be something special, he had to commit to doing something special.

"There are so many more talented people who are more athletic and could jump higher," he said. "My goal was that no one would ever outwork me."

His mission was a resounding success. Most important, said Larry Franks, was one trait that he found particularly endearing.

"Brian was never the obnoxious, 'I'm the star. I need the ball,' player," Franks said. "He never felt he was the star. He felt he was a part of it. He was easily coached and was never bigger than the team."

While his devotion and dedication were sincere and serious, Cardinal never lost his sense of humor.

Former high school teammate Joe O'Neill recalled how Cardinal would break the monotony when an opponent was preparing to shoot a free throw.

"He'd be at the other end of the court sometimes, but he'd yell out, 'I've got the shooter!' " O'Neill said.

Brian with his high school coaches, Gary Wilsey (left) and Dan Akers. *(Photo courtesy of Brian Cardinal)*

CHAPTER FIVE

Small Town, Big Ambitions

Tolono, Illinois, is not a mecca for aspiring athletes. It's not a community where collegiate coaches stop with regularity.

Yet, it is where Brian Cardinal was reared, where he first learned to sacrifice his body and dive on the floor, where he diligently worked on his perimeter shooting, where the basketball became his constant companion.

His accolades and accomplishments were impressive. As a freshman in 1991-92, he became the first ninth grader in the school's 43 years of existence to start on the varsity basketball team.

Brian was a double-figure scorer his final three years at Unity, carrying the Rockets at least as far as the sectional finals each season, while helping the school to a cumulative record of 76-11.

This was the same Unity program that had endured a 1-24 season the year before Brian Cardinal entered high school.

His reputation grew throughout the Illini Central Conference as well as all of east central Illinois.

"He was pretty much the centerpiece of everything we did," said former Unity teammate Eric Stevens. "We all worked hard to help him succeed as a player."

Beyond his immediate area, however, Cardinal was underrated and virtually unknown.

"I used to say we had the best-kept secret in the State of Illinois," said Gary Wilsey, who was then an assistant coach at Unity.

Wilsey's coaching career has taken him to Bridgeport (Illinois) and now on to Indiana's Mount Vernon High School, where he will become head coach beginning with the 2001-2002 season. His players can expect to see and hear about Cardinal.

"When kids think they are playing hard, I say, 'Let me show you this,' and I put in a tape of Brian so they can see what playing hard is. He plays the game the way most of us think it should be played."

Brian Cardinal was concerned that living in a community of 2,600 residents and attending a high school of 420 students would limit his college options.

"I wondered if I should have gone to Champaign Central or Centennial so I'd get more notoriety, more press coverage, and more people looking at me," Brian said. "My

Brian and his high school teammates reunite at the ceremoney retiring Brian's high school jersey. *(Photo courtesy of Brian Cardinal)*

thinking was that I was from a small town and nobody was going to know about the Tolono Rockets. I thought if I moved to a bigger town, which wasn't really that far from here, it might help."

Before the notion to transfer gained steam, Rod Cardinal spoke to his son.

"My dad told me that colleges will find you if you can play, no matter where you live," Brian said.

Nothing more needed to be said. The only moves Brian Cardinal would make before graduation would be on the hardwood.

Bruce Weber, a Purdue assistant when Cardinal was recruited, said Rod Cardinal's contention is probably right. Fewer players are overlooked today than 25 years ago.

"Because of the number of AAU [Amateur Athletic Union] teams and national camps, kids get exposure now at an earlier age," Weber said.

Wilsey left nothing to chance. He added marketing duties to the ones he had as coach.

"I felt all along he'd be something special," Wilsey said, "but we had to kind of force him onto people, recruiting-wise."

A highlight videotape was made, and copies were distributed to various coaches.

"We tried to sell him to people at first," Wilsey said. "It was the summer before his senior year that people took a serious interest in him."

There had already been signs of his growth. His final two years at Unity High School, Cardinal's uniform number was 55, not 35.

"My mom's cooking got better," he quipped, "and I outgrew the first one."

The tapes may have sparked interest, but Cardinal enhanced it by his play in camps and as a member of Larry Butler's AAU team.

Brian can pinpoint when the interest in him started to mushroom. He was a participant in Butler's Spotlight Shootout in Chicago in 1994.

"For some crazy reason, I played great, out of control," he said. "That's where I got spotted by colleges. It's where Purdue noticed me.

"It's where I started believing and thinking, 'Holy Cow! This dream I have of playing college ball might honestly happen.' "

Within a few short months, Brian Cardinal became one of the most coveted high school basketball players in the State of Illinois.

C H A P T E R   S I X

One of the Élite

Seeing is believing.

People who make their living as talent scouts, evaluating high school players and ranking them in their publications, became Cardinal fans en masse in 1994.

Hoop Scoop Newsletter, in its July 26, 1994, edition, rated the top 80 players (out of 120) at the ABCD Camp, in Teaneck, New Jersey. The publication stated that the ranking was based on camp performance, not college potential.

Brian Cardinal was listed at No. 29.

Among the campers ahead of him:

1. Robert Traylor
2. Sharif Abdur-Rahim

3. Stephon Marbury

6. Paul Pierce

14. Ryan Blackwell

18. Kobe Bryant

21. Mike Robinson

Of those listed above, all were upcoming high school seniors except for Bryant and Robinson, both a year younger. Robinson ultimately wound up as Cardinal's collegiate teammate. Blackwell was eventually recruited by the University of Illinois in place of Cardinal.

After his performance at the Adidas Summer Shootout in Columbus, Ohio, Cardinal was ranked as the 14th-best player in the August issue of *Reidell's Roundball Review*.

Later in the fall of 1994, *Hoop Scoop Basketball* publication placed Cardinal as the 24th-best senior in Illinois, saying, "Cardinal is strong, has great hands, protects the ball well, and has a good array of power moves around the basket."

After Thanksgiving, Cardinal's stock had risen even higher.

In the December 1, 1994, edition of *The Sporting News*, the St. Louis-based weekly listed Cardinal as one of "The Hot 100" senior basketball players in America.

He was ranked 78th.

Cardinal's reputation—and resume—grew after he was not only selected to an Adidas all-star team that toured Finland following his junior year at Unity, but was also a starter for a squad that was 6-0.

Life was changing, not just for Brian, but also for his family. The most unprepared for the onslaught of mail and telephone calls was his mother, Mary.

"He was getting stuff in the mail every day, just tons and tons of stuff, and all different kinds of schools were calling for him. I pretty much had to play the receptionist and screen calls for him," she said.

Though she enjoyed watching her children play sports, Mary Cardinal wasn't an overbearing parent who emphasized an athletic scholarship as the way to go to college.

"I never grew up around people who had gotten athletic scholarships," she said. "I wouldn't have dreamt in a million years that he would have gotten a scholarship. I was totally blown away."

There were daily reminders that she was wrong. Cards and letters filled the mailbox. The return addresses included Duke, Kansas, Miami (Florida), Michigan, Minnesota,

Northwestern, Penn State, Pittsburgh, Stetson, UCLA, Vanderbilt, Wisconsin, and—of course—Purdue.

"It was not necessarily a 'Who's Who in Basketball,' but it was certainly an impressive listing of people who would make their weekly phone calls," Rod Cardinal said.

"The recruiting was crazy."

Most schools used different methods to make themselves seem enticing and irresistible. Rod Cardinal said one of the most creative letters came from Miami (Florida).

"Theirs was, imagine as you come to the game, you walk past palm trees and hear the ocean and walk past their version of the Illinettes and come out on the floor to hear 16,000 people chanting, 'Brian! Brian!' " he said.

"They tried to build the story line. Some were pretty neat, the thought that went into it. Some were kind of funny and a lot of them were pretty danged serious, too."

After sorting through materials from 61 schools that persistently pursued Brian, the Cardinals scheduled home visits with six institutions.

Brian's three finalists were Purdue, Penn State and Vanderbilt. On November 10, 1994—approximately two weeks before the start of his senior season—Brian Cardinal

ended the speculation and signed a letter of intent with
Purdue University.

Brian blowing out the candles on his 16th birthday.
Wishing for a career in the NBA? (Photo courtesy of Brian
Cardinal)

C H A P T E R   S E V E N

Overlooked by the illini

Hindsight gives us all 20-20 vision.

In retrospect, it is easy to accuse the University of Illinois of missing out on a potential star by not actively recruiting Brian Cardinal, the son of the school's veteran men's basketball trainer.

The reasons for the conclusion are obvious and go far beyond the Illini losing to Cardinal's Purdue Boilermakers all eight times they played while he was in uniform.

At Purdue, Cardinal became the school's all-time leader in games started (125) and helped the Boilermakers reach at least the Sweet 16 in the NCAA playoffs three consecu-

(Photo courtesy of Gold and Black Illustrated)

tive years and a cumulative record of 75-31 for those seasons.

His senior season, Purdue advanced to the Elite Eight, where it lost to Wisconsin.

Lou Henson, who started his 22-year tenure as the Illinois head basketball coach in 1975, was well aware of Brian Cardinal.

"Even as a youngster, he was totally committed to the game of basketball, was so enthusiastic and had a keen interest in the game," said Henson, now the head coach at New Mexico State University.

"We thought he would be a very good player. Then he exceeded most people's expectations. I don't think anybody, including myself, thought he would go out and impact games like he did. Brian was a warrior. He would fight you."

Henson said it was a difficult decision not to recruit Cardinal.

"Brian comes from a good family, but I didn't know how soon he could play, and if it would be a good situation," Henson said. "Had he been someplace else and had Rod not been there, we would have recruited him.

"How many people wouldn't have recruited a 6-8 kid who is a very good student and dedicated to the game? Some of the time, young men and young women are better off to get away from home.

"I've never worked with anyone I enjoyed working with more than his dad, but I think we were trying to do what was best for Brian," said Henson.

The Illini never offered a scholarship to Cardinal.

Who can say Cardinal would have thrived at Illinois like he did at Purdue? Who can say he would have found the same niche, or that his press clippings wouldn't have proven too burdensome?

Brian with Purdue coaches Bruce Weber (left) and Gene Keady. (*Photo courtesy of Brian Cardinal*)

"I don't know if I would have gone to Illinois, but it would have been nice just to have had the opportunity to say it was down to Illinois and Purdue, or that Illinois is not in the picture," Brian Cardinal said.

"I don't hold anything against those guys or the university. I wouldn't change anything, good or bad. Everything that has happened, I totally think it was for the best."

He'd get no argument from his mother. Mary Cardinal has no regrets about Illinois' lack of interest in her son.

"I wasn't disappointed at all," she said. "In fact, I don't think we would have wanted him to go there regardless. It was an issue for everybody else, but it was never an issue for us."

She knew the scrutiny an area player would receive at Illinois, as well as the expectations that would accompany him. Comments made on radio call-in programs can range from complimentary to degrading.

"It would have been real difficult listening to people criticizing Brian," she said. "We got that even when he was over at Purdue, and you get real defensive when it's your own kids."

Rod Cardinal understands the reasons, yet it was hard for him to be convinced.

"Early on, I was disappointed, because we liked Coach Henson so much, and Brian had been so involved with them (as a former ball boy)," he said.

"We never realized or dreamt the guy would make an All-Big Ten player and make a couple All-USA basketball teams. The way things turned out, sure. Now, it's like money in the bank. You know he was successful, you know he graduated and had a lot of fun and was certainly appreciated at Purdue.

"Probably up until his senior year, there

Perimeter shooting became a strength for Brian. (Photo courtesy of Gold and Black Illustrated)

was a part of me that said, 'I wish he was here. I wish I could work with him every day and be part of his growth and development.' It was hard to take at first, but more and more as we look back, Coach Henson probably had the right idea."

Purdue coach Gene Keady, known for his sense of humor, reported mixed feelings whenever his Boilermakers played the Illini.

"I sort of felt sorry for his mother," Keady said. "If we beat Illinois, her husband might get fired. If we lose, I might cut Brian."

Keady said Cardinal's character was a big reason he put an emphasis on his recruitment.

"In his mind, I don't think he thought he was that good," Keady said. "He always played with extra effort and extra energy. He loved to play."

Keady was unprepared for the magnitude of the impact Cardinal would make.

"Once we got him here and saw how good he was, I was surprised we got him away from Illinois," he said.

Keady's recruiting visit to the Cardinal residence was one of the family's most memorable.

"The first thing he said was, 'What is going on with Illinois? Why aren't they involved?' " Rod Cardinal related.

The situation was explained to the veteran coach, and he responded, "Their loss will be my gain."

Rod Cardinal took advantage of that opening to ask a question.

"I said, 'Does that mean you're going to offer a scholarship?' and he said, 'I wouldn't be sitting in this chair if I didn't think it was going to be worth it,' " Rod Cardinal recalled.

"He was trying to be gruff but turned out to be one of the funniest comedians you'd ever want in the house."

Although Illinois didn't recruit his son, Rod Cardinal said the school's assistants at the time, especially Jimmy Collins, Dick Nagy and Mark Coomes, offered valuable help.

"They were advocates of Coach Henson recruiting Brian," Rod Cardinal said. "They felt like he could be a contributor. They weren't able to convince Coach that would actually be the fact, but they were instrumental in getting Brian invited to the ABCD camp in New Jersey, and others, for exposure."

Coomes, who has been on staff at Illinois-Chicago the past five years, had taken a position at Wabash Valley Community College in Mount Carmel, Illinois, before the start of Cardinal's senior year at Unity High School.

"There was no question in my mind he could play in the Big Ten," Coomes said. "He was always aggressive, hard-working, had shooting touch and size.

"When you put that in a package with his redshirt year, I'm not surprised. I felt he'd be a good college player at a high level, but you couldn't predict that he'd be as good as he was."

Playing on the court took on new meaning when Brian was in the game. (Photo courtesy of Gold and Black Illustrated)

CHAPTER EIGHT

Feeling Lost and Overwhelmed

He was not alone. He just felt like it.

Within weeks of graduating from Unity High School, Brian moved into an apartment in West Lafayette, Indiana.

The teenager was anxious to get oriented to Purdue University and the surroundings that would be his collegiate home the next five years.

Brian shared an apartment with Brad Miller (now with the Chicago Bulls in the NBA) and Paul Gilvydis, both of whom were members of the men's basketball team.

"I knew no one except guys on the team, and they already had people they knew," Brian recalled.

"I was stuck in an apartment with no cable [television]. I was a mess."

He could tolerate a boring social life, because that was not the reason he was on campus. Basketball brought Cardinal to Purdue. Basketball would be his salvation. That was his thought during the hours he spent tucked away in his room, wondering about his future.

When he played in his first open gym, Brian said, "I was scared to death."

He was almost relieved not to be one of the top choices when Purdue players picked sides for an informal scrimmage following a summer camp session.

Many of the budding prospects remained courtside to get an up-close look at the Boilermakers in action. The incoming freshmen—Cardinal, Luther Clay (who later transferred after one year at Purdue), and Alan Eldridge—were part of a recruiting class that was ranked 10th nationally.

The pickup game ended soon enough, but Cardinal's night did not.

"I heard 'Brian,' and I went out to replace someone," he said.

Years later, the minutes that followed remained as clear in his mind as if they had occurred only yesterday.

"I played one of the worst games of my life," Brian said. "I shot an air ball, I threw the ball away, and Matt Waddell made the winning shot on me."

It was a traumatic time for a youth away from home. He desperately needed confidence and acceptance. The only feeling growing inside Brian during the summer of '95 was uncertainty.

"I was crying as I drove back to the apartment that night," he said. "I laid on the bed and said, 'What am I doing here? I'm the dumbest person in the world to think I could make it at Purdue. I had offers to go to smaller schools and I could have been decent.' "

Word about Cardinal's unofficial debut circulated quickly. The phone at his apartment rang shortly after he arrived.

It was Purdue basketball assistant Bruce Weber. It was the start of a longstanding friendship. Brian Cardinal talked candidly to Coach Weber.

"I don't know what I'm doing here," he blurted out to Weber.

The coach understood. Freshmen are predictable. They all fall into the same basic category.

They arrive a little cocky and self-assured because they were the stars of their high school teams. They are not ready for the drastic difference in the level of play.

Freshmen simply expect to pick up in college where they left off in high school. It rarely happens.

Weber understood.

"He doubted himself," Weber said. "He thought there was no way he could play in the Big Ten, and that he was out of place."

They talked. For more than an hour, they were on the phone. Brian spoke from his heart.

"I was petrified of ever stepping foot back in the gym," he said.

Weber tried to convince the new recruit that he wasn't expected to be an immediate superstar.

His manner was calm. His tone was relaxed. His words were compelling. Cardinal was becoming convinced.

"I knew he would help me out and wouldn't lead me astray," Cardinal said.

Rod Cardinal said what his son needed most in his first months at Purdue was positive reinforcement.

"This was a huge step for him," Rod Cardinal said. "At that point, he needed reassurance he wasn't a wasted scholarship, that he wasn't a filler."

Cardinal knew Weber was someone whom he could trust. It became a two-way street. Their relationship evolved from player and coach to friends.

"He talked to my wife and played with my girls," Weber said.

Four years later, when Weber left Purdue to become head coach at Southern Illinois University at Carbondale, Cardinal was devastated.

"I knew this was a great move for him," Cardinal said, "but this was the guy who kept my head on my shoulders. He was my savior.

"I honestly cried because he was leaving me."

Weber was the coach who was instrumental in recruiting Cardinal. He was fond of Cardinal as a person as well as an athlete.

"He was a regular student athlete, somebody you enjoyed coaching, somebody who was always willing to learn," Weber said.

C H A P T E R   N I N E

The Name Game

Throughout the history of sports, there are athletes as well known by their nicknames as their given names.

True sports fans can readily identify The Sultan of Swat as Babe Ruth, The Georgia Peach as Ty Cobb, The Splendid Splinter as Ted Williams, and Air as Michael Jordan.

Thanks to a teenage basketball fan in West Lafayette, Indiana, Purdue University forward Brian Cardinal will forever be associated with the nickname "Citizen Pain."

Zac Laugheed, then 13, was doing homework one February night in 1997. His 22-year-old brother Sam was watching one of his favorite movies, "Citizen Kane."

An item in the local newspaper, the *Lafayette Journal and Courier*, caught Zac's attention.

DEFENSE WINS!
(Photos courtesy of Gold and Black Illustrated)

There was a "Name the Freshman" contest, and readers were asked to submit entries for an appropriate moniker for Brian, who was a redshirt freshman less than three months into his career as a Boilermaker.

"We're avid Purdue fans," said Zac, who teamed up with his brother for nearly two dozen entries.

"We figured the best one was 'Citizen Pain,' but I wasn't sure what the response would be," Zac said.

Before a five-member panel made its selection, more than 260 responses had been reviewed. Entries arrived from eight states, including as far away as Arizona.

Former high school teammate Eric Stevens wasn't surprised by Cardinal's popularity.

"After that first year, with all his hard work, I knew he'd be an icon," Stevens said, "but it was pretty insane to hear Dick Vitale talk about Brian as one of the hardest-working players he'd seen. He was talking about a friend we'd known since kindergarten."

Laugheed's submission of "Citizen Pain" was the winning entry, beating out "Rawhide" and "The Janitor."

The common theme among the top three choices was an attempt to describe Cardinal's fearless, kamikaze style of play.

"Citizen Pain." *(Photo courtesy of Gold and Black Illustrated)*

"He'd go through anything," said Laugheed, who tried to pattern his aggressive play after Cardinal's.

"I'd go in the stands to get the ball," said Laugheed, whose own basketball career ended after his freshman year when he decided to concentrate on track and field, and his specialty, the pole vault, at Harrison High School.

Laugheed was less surprised that his entry won than he was by its permanence.

"I thought it would be a one-week deal," he said, "but then I read it in *Sports Illustrated* and saw it on ESPN."

One of the sports writers at the Lafayette newspaper, Jeff Washburn, has a lifetime of Purdue memories. Washburn has been the Purdue beat writer for nine years and has followed the Boilermakers almost 40 years.

"Other than Rick Mount (1968-70) and Glenn Robinson (1993-94), Brian Cardinal was the most popular player, because of the way he played," Washburn said.

"It was not a surprise we'd get that kind of response. A lot of fans related to him. Everyone was so impressed with his grit and how he dove on the floor. Fans would write letters to the editor on how much they enjoyed watching him play."

The typical image of Cardinal was of Brian wearing knee pads and elbow pads, with his hair out of place, a bandage on his nose, and his body covered with cuts, scrapes, and bruises.

"He inflicted pain on opponents as well as himself," Washburn said.

"A lot of credit has to go to Coach [Gene] Keady for developing a role Brian could play," Rod Cardinal said. "The coaches helped formulate this person as a tough, bruising, take-no-prisoners basketball player. The thing that differentiates Brian from others is that it had to be that way for every practice, every road game and every home game."

A subsequent newspaper story on Laugheed included a photo of the then-Klondike Middle School student wrapped up like a mummy, and comments from Cardinal that he liked the winning entry best of the five finalists.

Cardinal had no say in the matter.

"I didn't vote," he said.

Four years after the contest, the nickname remains.

"People see me who know my name, but they'll say, 'Citizen Pain,'" Cardinal said.

CHAPTER TEN

'Shut Up and Listen'

Brian Cardinal may have been the Golden Boy in the eyes of Purdue fans, but he was hardly immune from the wrath of the coaching staff.

He was the target of as much criticism as his teammates.

"He got yelled at a lot more than anyone on the team," said Jay Price, a Purdue assistant. "Coach [Gene Keady] was on him a lot, but Brian could take it.

"So many times we'd have to knock him around and yell at him."

Keady said Cardinal brought on some of the vocal outbursts himself.

(Photo courtesy of Gold and Black Illustrated)

"Brian was a 'Why' guy," Keady said. "I'm more of a 'Shut up and listen' guy. Once he quit asking, 'What if?' once he got over that, he turned into a great player.

"His junior year, he forgot about it and played."

Cardinal's first year on campus (1995-96) resulted in a redshirt season. He was withheld from games, preserving his four years of eligibility.

"Redshirting was 60 percent their idea and 40 percent mine," Brian said.

He practiced regularly and traveled with the team, but he was not allowed to play in the games.

Once the decision was made to redshirt, Cardinal made sure Keady received reminders during road trips.

"I'd knock on his door before away games and say, 'Don't play me tonight,' " Cardinal related. "He'd say, 'Shut up, get dressed and get taped. I might put you in.'

"I was scared to death he'd put me in a game. I might make a shot once every 10 times, but the other nine, I'd probably shoot an air ball or over the backboard."

Although he didn't think Keady was serious about playing him that season, Cardinal wasn't positive.

"I knew I didn't want to get out there and play, but some of the guys weren't playing as well as Coach wanted,

Who is doing the coaching? Brian, whose basketball knowledge is considered superb, joins Purdue coach Gene Keady in instructing players. (Photo courtesy of Gold and Black Illustrated)

and I thought they were going to screw me up," Cardinal said.

Fortunately for Cardinal, the veteran team improved its play the second half of the season, and he was able to remain on the bench. At his power forward position, Purdue had seven players, three of whom were seniors.

Keady didn't think it would have hurt the team had Cardinal played. Following one preseason workout, he told Jeff Washburn of the *Lafayette Journal and Courier*, "After the scrimmage Saturday, he may be the best player on the team."

Cardinal's support of his teammates never wavered. Cardinal, in fact, referred to himself as the "bench captain" during the 1995-96 season.

"From Day 1, when he wasn't playing, he'd stand up and cheer and wave the towel," Jay Price said. "He had so much enthusiasm, fans fell in love with him."

It wasn't until the season ended that Keady learned Cardinal sometimes wore his warm-up top—but no game jersey—at games, and other times didn't get his ankles taped, all of which reduced the likelihood of his being able to play.

"He was a piece of work," Keady said. "He made everything comical."

During his redshirt year, Cardinal considered transferring. His thoughts were based on concerns about his ability to contribute, not due to animosity with the coaching staff.

"I called a junior college in Florida," Cardinal said, "because there were times I didn't think I was capable of playing at this level. After I got through the redshirt year, I calmed down mentally and relaxed and adjusted to the traveling."

He still keeps in touch with his former Purdue coaches.

"Coach Keady is one of my best friends," Cardinal said. "He's one of the greatest people I've ever met, as far as how genuine he is. People see him throw a coat on the sidelines or when his face gets red, but off the court, he's a great guy you can have a good conversation with.

"He and [former Purdue assistant Bruce] Weber are like my father figures."

For all the highlights, Cardinal can't shake the memory of what he considered a lowlight.

"We wanted to get Coach that missing piece to the puzzle. We wanted to be able to get him to the Final Four,"

Brian said. "At our senior banquet, I spoke and told him even though we weren't able to get him that missing piece, he had a piece of my heart, because I loved him so much."

Weber said Cardinal's performance improved once he started to believe in himself.

"He was not a very confident kid," Weber said. "As he got more confidence, he got better and better as a player. He used his strengths and he worked on his limitations.

"You hear people say Class A [small-school] kids can't play in the Big Ten. Brian definitely proved that theory wrong."

Brian Cardinal was a small-town athlete who became a big-time player.

(Photo courtesy of Gold and Black Illustrated)

C H A P T E R 11 E L E V E N

The Official Word

Long before he was a ballplayer, Brian Cardinal was a ball boy.

It was during his preteen years. Along with his older brother Troy—and years later, his younger sister Lisa—he'd go along with Dad to University of Illinois men's basketball games.

Rod Cardinal's three children were not only frequent visitors to UI men's practices (Troy once said, "Practice was our day care; one of us was probably at every practice for five or six years in a row"), but they were also there on game night.

Their actual duties as ball boys were minimal and had stopped by the time the boys entered high school.

"From their standpoint, it meant mingling with players in the locker room and hanging around and talking to them when they were getting ready for the games," Rod Cardinal said. "Their other duties were wiping off the floor and getting the officials a drink of water."

Years later, when he was playing at Purdue University, Brian Cardinal found that his strong relationship with referees was well established.

"It started when I was a ball boy and got them a towel or water and talked to them during timeouts," Brian Cardinal said. "A lot of those guys remembered me.

"Early on, I didn't get many calls, but as my career continued, my relationship with the refs grew because they knew I respected them for what they did. Even though I was talking to them, it was out of respect."

When Purdue was on road trips, Cardinal was often viewed as the villain, the one player whom opposing crowds loved to hate. He described himself as "looking a little goofy," and he was ridiculed for his appearance (a full assortment of pads and, eventually, a receding hairline) and subjected to countless boos.

"The fans were mad at me because I was doing something successful to help my team," Cardinal said.

Guess what?

The reaction had an effect on the young player, but not the one those sellout crowds would have hoped for.

"I relished stuff like that and it motivated me," Cardinal said. "I took it that I must be doing something right for my team. I'd rather they yelled at me than one of my teammates, because I knew I could take it."

The only time Cardinal felt unjustly accused, and the occasion when his anger reached the surface, was in 1998, when CBS television commentator Sean McDonough cited unnamed Big Ten Conference coaches who called Cardinal a "dirty player."

Back home in Tolono, folks were upset.

"He's a competitor and the type of kid you love if he's on your team, but a dirty player? That aggravated us," summer coach Larry Franks said.

Cardinal said his play spoke for itself.

"If that was the case [that he was a dirty player], the refs would have stopped it," he said, "but they never did. That was ridiculous."

(Photo courtesy of Gold and Black Illustrated)

He later made a public statement to convey his feelings.

"My quote was that if there was a loose ball, I was going to try to get it," he said.

"I'd go through a brick wall to try to get it for my team. I had a will to win. If that makes me a dirty player, then I'm the dirtiest player that ever was."

(Photo courtesy of Gold and Black Illustrated)

C H A P T E R   T W E L V E

Summer Fun

During the off-season at Purdue, Brian Cardinal spent his time in a familiar pursuit. He played basketball.

In May 1996, he played on a select team, called "People to People Sports," which played 10 games against international competition. The squad was 8-2, including 7-0 on a tour of Spain.

They were 1-2 in Prague, the Czech Republic.

Cardinal was a power forward who had 52 points, 37 rebounds, 17 assists, and 14 steals on the trip.

A year later, he had to be convinced to try out for a USA Basketball team, which featured many of the nation's elite 22-and-under collegians.

Rick Majerus, now the coach at Utah, put 61 prospects through a series of practices before he picked a 12-member team, which included Cardinal.

The team played in Melbourne, Australia, in July 1997. Cardinal became a starter and helped the Americans win six of eight games to place fifth.

Jim Tooley, now the executive director of USA Basketball, wasn't shocked.

"Talent-wise, he wasn't one of the top kids there, but he outworked so many people and had good fundamentals that people took notice," Tooley said. "It was impressive to see.

"He is one of my favorite kids who ever came through here [Colorado Springs, site of the tryouts]," Tooley said. "His attitude was one of the best, if not the best.

"What a great ambassador for U.S. basketball."

Cardinal's exemplary attitude surfaced the next summer when he made another prestigious all-star team.

Along with athletes such as Elton Brand and Wally Szczerbiak, Cardinal made a team that was coached by Clem Haskins and competed in the 1998 Goodwill Games in New York.

(Photo courtesy of Brian Cardinal)

Having teammates who are now firmly entrenched in the NBA made a bigger impression on Cardinal later than it did during the competition.

"At the time, I thought it was just another team," he said.

Cardinal's playing time was limited to 17 minutes in four games.

"He was the 12th man on the team," Tooley said, "but he never moped or felt sorry for himself. When guys came off the floor, he was the first one giving them high fives.

"He understood not all 12 could play, and he made the experience a great one. We've found, on a number of our teams, that the 11th and 12th players can be detrimental. He was anything but that. I think the world of him."

His ultimate reward was a gold medal from the Goodwill Games, where his team went 4-1.

A lecture from his father, when Cardinal was coping as a redshirt at Purdue, helped him recognize the satisfaction that comes from being part of a team.

"I know how difficult it can be to work so hard and have absolutely nothing to show for it," Rod Cardinal said. "I told him to trust the coach and don't be a problem.

"I said if there's going to be a problem, let it be some of the other people. Just deal with it."

His attitude during the tournament in New York was exemplary. Cardinal recognized the talent on the USA team and where he stood in comparison.

"At halftime of one of the games, I went up to one of the coaches and said, 'Don't play me,' " Cardinal said.

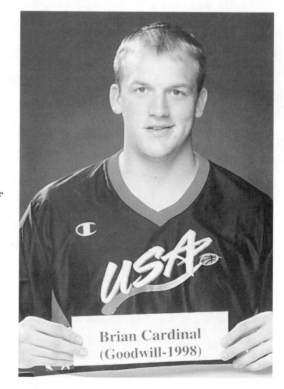

(Photo courtesy of Brian Cardinal)

By the time his comment had sunk in to the staff member, Cardinal was explaining his feelings.

"In order for us to have a chance to win, everyone can't play the same amount of minutes," he said. "I'll sacrifice for the team to try to win the gold medal.

"My role was to keep everyone's spirits high. I cheered and helped lead from the bench."

The 1998 Goodwill Games team. Elton Brand is No. 11, Wally Szczerbiak is No. 10 and Brian is No. 13. (Photo courtesy of Brian Cardinal)

CHAPTER 13 THIRTEEN

Road to the Pros

To many, they are simply words: Professional basketball.

It's the ultimate dream for many youngsters from the time they first lace up a pair of sneakers.

Brian Cardinal was aware of the play-for-pay game but never dwelled on it.

"The first time I seriously thought about it was a third to halfway through my senior year in college," Brian said. "That's when I thought, 'Maybe I can play.' "

An internship in 1998 with a pharmaceutical company in New Jersey (Scherring Plough) provided an indication of what life in the real world would be like without sports.

Brian then decided he wasn't ready yet for that phase of his life to begin.

When Brian had the opportunity to leave resumes for companies at a job seminar his senior year, he found himself hesitant. He went to the seminar dressed in a suit and tie, prepared to meet and greet prospective employers.

"I got my name tag on, but I was so nervous I stood in the doorway for 40 minutes," Brian said. "I knew I had to get a job after I graduated, but at that point, my thinking was, what do I have to offer?

"In the 41st minute, I said, 'I've got to get out of here.' "

He returned home, still carrying all of the resumes he had brought.

He may have been unsure of what he had to offer in the real world, but basketball coaches were not in a similar dilemma.

When the 2000 NBA draft was held, Cardinal was a second-round pick of the Detroit Pistons. He was the 44th player overall to be drafted.

Cardinal watched the draft on television from his West Lafayette apartment with his parents, his sister, girlfriend, and a roomful of friends.

They dined on chicken wings from C-Ray's, where Brian had worked one summer as a waiter; pizza from Bruno's, and waited.

There was a sense of anticipation, but it was unlike Christmastime, when there was bound to be something he liked.

"There were so many questions, there were absolutely no answers to," Cardinal said. "Will I get drafted or not? Will it be a good fit? I didn't know what might happen."

The so-called draft analysts were of little help. Some said Cardinal would get picked in the first round. Others projected him as a second-round selection. Some even said he would not get drafted.

Brian felt like he was on a roller coaster as the draft progressed. His feelings would soar. Then they would plummet.

"Some people were drafted, and I was like, 'I'm as good as him,' " Cardinal said.

When his name was finally flashed on the TV screen at 10:08 p.m. as the choice of the Detroit Pistons, Brian remembers his mother crying and the room "going crazy."

He hardly had time to collect his thoughts before "the phone rang, then my cell phone rang, and all of a sudden I was bombarded by calls."

Though he had grown up following the Chicago Bulls and the Indiana Pacers, Cardinal was diplomatic when talking about his new team.

"I've always liked them," he said. "I just don't know a lot about them."

That would change soon.

Certainly, he was considered a long shot to make the NBA team, but for Cardinal, that was better than no shot at all.

"I've learned you don't ever tell Brian Cardinal he can't do something," said Troy Cardinal, his older brother.

Prior to the draft, Cardinal helped himself with his performances at two open tournaments.

He was one of 54 players at the Portsmouth (Virginia) Invitational on April 8, 2000. He averaged 13.3 points and 8.0 rebounds.

Seventy-two hours later, he was in Phoenix for the Nike Desert Classic. Forty prospects were there. Brian averaged 7.7 points and 5.3 rebounds.

On Draft Day, he was the highest Purdue athlete to be selected since 1994, when Glenn Robinson was the No. 1 overall pick (by the Milwaukee Bucks).

George Irvine was coaching Detroit at the time of the 2000 draft, but followed Cardinal's collegiate career while working for the Indiana Pacers.

"If you see him on one occasion, you might not notice him," Irvine said. "He's not a pretty player. He doesn't jump over a bunch of people and dunk the ball, but he's the kind of guy you appreciate when you watch him day in and day out."

He takes charges, sets screens, knocks balls loose and blocks out.

"People look at talent level, but having a great work ethic and being tough-minded can take you a long way," Irvine said. "He does a lot of little things well. Coaches and teammates appreciate him.

"Knowing there's a guy on the bench who will go in and play hard is invaluable. You can never have too many Brian Cardinals on a team."

Brian played in 15 of the Pistons' 82 games as a rookie, averaging 8.4 minutes, 2.1 points and 1.5 rebounds per game.

After an April 2001 game against the Toronto Raptors, Detroit guard Chucky Atkins told Booth News Service sports writer A. Sherrod Blakely,

"People don't really know how good Brian is, because he hasn't really gotten a chance to play a lot this year. If he was given the minutes, he would really produce for us."

Whether he was playing 21 minutes (his season high) or not at all, Cardinal was content.

"I'm just a guy who is low on the totem pole. I won't be a star in the NBA," Brian said. "I'm happy to be the last man on the bench."

A few months after the NBA draft, an irony surfaced when the Continental Basketball Association held its 16th annual draft on September 19, 2000.

Cardinal was the No. 3 selection. The LaCrosse (Wisconsin) Bobcats picked him.

The No. 1 pick was Ryan Blackwell, who grew up in Champaign, but moved to New York before starting high school. The 6-7 Blackwell originally signed with Illinois, but transferred to Syracuse, where he started all 100 games in which he played.

Dodge City of the United States Basketball League also drafted Cardinal.

Before he signed with the Pistons, Brian also received additional offers to play professionally in Italy and Turkey.

Brian chatting with former IU coach Bobby Knight. *(Photo courtesy of Gold and Black Illustrated)*

C H A P T E R   F O U R T E E N

Starting Over, Again and Again

Basketball had been Brian Cardinal's passion for years.

Yet all of his awards, knowledge, and court recognition meant little when he signed to play in the NBA.

Once again, he was starting over. He was in the position of needing to prove that he belonged. His previous exploits weren't going to impress the pros.

Entering a league where the size of egos sometimes matches the size of salaries, Cardinal didn't know what to expect.

"I was worried that no one would talk to me," he said. "I was scared that I would get laughed out of there.

(Photo courtesy of Einstein Photos)

"Instead, it was totally the opposite."

It wasn't just rookies—other players in his similar circumstance—who made him feel comfortable and accepted. Veterans such as Jud Buechler, who played for the Chicago Bulls during their NBA championship threepeat from 1996 to 1998, and Jerome Williams were in his corner.

"Jud and I bonded," Cardinal said. "He saw a lot of himself in me. He looked at me from the standpoint of where he was 10 or 11 years back.

"I was green, unsure of my own ability, and scared, but he helped me make sure I wasn't too mentally exhausted. He showed me the ropes and showed me where the good dining spots were."

Cardinal soon learned that his player's $89 per diem for meals could go quickly if he weren't careful.

"I had to get used to the amount of money people spend," Cardinal said. "Sometimes at these restaurants it costs $60 or $70 for one person. Some of these places, I wouldn't go to if I weren't in the NBA."

Buechler has been a fixture in the league since 1991. That in itself was reason enough for Cardinal to use him as a role model.

(Photo courtesy of Einstein Photos)

"Even though he got traded [to Phoenix], our friendship will continue to grow," Cardinal said. "I owe a lot to him."

Buechler said it was easy to take a liking to Cardinal.

"His attitude toward the game and toward practices reminded me of the old days when guys were proud and honored to play in the NBA," Buechler said. "That has changed a lot. Rookies come out now and think the NBA should be doing cartwheels to have them come out.

"I've seen a lot of rookies come in, and last year with Detroit, from the top player to the trainer, Brian was immediately liked. People wanted to see him do well. A lot of that has to do with his personality and style of play."

Williams and Cardinal used to share rides when the team would go from its training site in Auburn Hills, Michigan, to the airport in Detroit, a 45-minute trip. Their friendship started because of their similar work ethics.

"He not only helped develop my basketball game, but also helped develop myself and helped the transition [to professional ball] go smoothly," Cardinal said.

Professional accommodations were unlike any Cardinal could have imagined. The Pistons have their own team plane, which he said has "leather couches and leather re-cliners."

Meals are served on board, but not standard fare, such as pretzels, peanuts, and soda pop.

"The food was amazing," Cardinal said. "There are huge fruit baskets and huge vegetable trays."

That was merely the appetizer.

"Then you have a choice of two salads, two or three soups, two or three entrees and two or three desserts. You eat well on the plane."

Hotel rooms are reserved at places such as the Ritz-Carlton, "places I'd drive by until I got to one where I was paying $50 a night," Cardinal said, referring to times when he traveled by himself.

Each player has his own room, which features a king-sized bed and over a half-dozen pillows.

"It's so comfortable you melt away and instantly fall asleep," Cardinal said.

The security can be short-lived, however. A player can feel at home but suddenly find himself traded. Cardinal dealt with that reality as a rookie when Jerome Williams was dealt to Toronto.

(Photo courtesy of Einstein Photos)

"That's the business," Cardinal said. "If you want security, NBA basketball is not the job to get into.

"One minute you think you have stability, friends, neighbors, and you're settled, and the next moment you're packing a bag to move and be somewhere else in 24 or 48 hours. They make additions, and sometimes they have to make subtractions."

For all Cardinal knows, he could be that person later today or maybe tomorrow.

"If the worst thing is that you get traded a couple of times, you're still in the NBA," he said. "The pros far outweigh the cons.

"This is truly a business, and even though this is the greatest job in the world, it was one of the first real shocks for me."

Cardinal's most embarrassing moment as a rookie occurred the night in December when he was activated from the disabled list. He was sidelined much of his rookie season with patella tendinitis in his left knee.

The pregame meetings at Portland's Rose Garden had ended, and the Pistons were preparing to take the floor to warm up.

"Stack [Jerry Stackhouse] nudges me and says, 'We want you to lead the team out,' " Cardinal recalled. "The ball boy threw me a ball, and I was feeling good.

"I get to half-court and look around, and no one is around me. Everyone is back in the tunnel, laughing up a storm. They were ruthless to me."

It could have been worse, Williams said.

"I got it as well [as a rookie]," Williams said, "except they did it to me in Detroit."

(Photo courtesy of Gold and Black Illustrated)

C H A P T E R FIFTEEN

Unchanged by Success

Basketball has taken Brian Cardinal to more places than the inside of steamy gymnasiums on sultry summer days.

The game has enabled him to travel.

"I've seen the world—Australia, Spain, Finland, France —all through basketball," he said. "It has been awesome."

Family and friends offer the ultimate compliments as they speak about a person they've known for more than two decades.

Joe O'Neill was a teammate of Brian's for years, graduating from Unity in 1994. Their friendship revolved around more than sports. O'Neill found Cardinal to be a considerate, caring person.

"We talk at least once a month, and he always wants to know how my family is doing," said O'Neill, a business systems analyst for Metris, a Minneapolis-based credit card company.

Mary Cardinal is naturally proud of her son. Her feelings aren't restricted to how he has performed on a basketball court.

"He never gave you the impression he was anything more special than the average person," she said. "He always looked out for the other guy and never had airs about him. He has always been a sensitive, tenderhearted kid, with a big heart.

"You'd never know what kind of job he had by talking to him or looking at him. He is still the same person. He never calls without telling us he loves us. He sends notes and cards, and the things he writes are just unbelievable. Some of the stuff he says is from his heart, so I know he'll never change."

When a game ended, Mary Cardinal's concern wasn't how many points or rebounds her son had that night.

"Sportsmanship was important," she said, "and making sure he didn't hog the ball."

Family and childhood friends aren't the only people who think highly of Brian Cardinal. Former NBA teammate Jerome Williams, who is now with Toronto, said Brian is "a class act and has a way about him that makes you feel at ease," and added, "if there were more guys like him in the NBA, we'd be the No. 1 sport in the world."

Now that Brian Cardinal has achieved success and recognition through basketball, one of his boyhood dreams has become reality. Youngsters now ask for his autograph. Brian willingly obliges each request.

"I sign every autograph people ever want," he said. "I truly love to sign. It's not a distraction."

As for his future, he hopes it includes many more years of competitive basketball. His long-term interests include one many would not expect.

"I'd love someday to own a farm," Cardinal said. "I don't know anything about planting, but I worked on a farm off and on throughout college every summer.

"Every day seems like a new day. A lot of people work 9 to 5 and do a similar job each day. On the farm, every day is a new challenge."

The farm idea might not be so far-fetched.

"My dad [Gene] said Brian was the best worker he ever had," said Gary Wilsey, a former Unity assistant coach whose father farmed near Sidney, Illinois.

Challenges are something Brian has never shied away from. He likes to meet them head-on.

Rod Cardinal has ideas of his own about his son.

"With his gift of gab, he ought to have been a politician," Rod Cardinal said. "He always has a story to tell."

Like the time in May 1997, when Brian Cardinal and members of Purdue's men's basketball team were in London, visiting Buckingham Palace.

Brian asked a sentry to blink if taking a picture was permissible. After receiving his signal, he snapped the picture and thanked the guard.

When he was greeted by silence, Cardinal chirped, "Blink if you want to thank me."

That comment prompted a smile from the sentry, according to Purdue assistant coach Jay Price.

"He's very friendly and open and has the ability to put people around him at ease," Rod Cardinal said. "He used to umpire at the park district for Little League baseball.

"He was able to disarm, so to speak, coaches who would get fired up over a call or a miscall. Brian was one of the more popular umpires we had for his ability to interact with coaches and make them feel comfortable."

(Photo courtesy of Gold and Black Illustrated)

C H A P T E R 16 S I X T E E N

Looking Ahead, and Back

What's next for Brian Cardinal?

His hope, of course, is to continue making a living by playing basketball.

If you believe what was written in Detroit newspapers after the 2000-01 season, it may be realistic to think he will stay in the NBA.

The *Detroit Free Press* graded all players at season's end. Among them, Mateen Cleaves, Dana Barros, Mikki Moore, Joe Smith, and Chucky Atkins all received C-minuses.

Cardinal was given a C.

Sports writer Perry A. Farrell wrote: "The young guy made a name for himself and is a keeper. Tough, dedicated and willing to mix it up, he has the perfect attitude for a blue-collar team."

In a subsequent interview, Farrell talked about why he liked Cardinal.

"He's like a gnat you swat at but can't get your hands on," Farrell said. "He's one of those guys that when it's time to practice, he more than held his own."

Veteran teammates took notice of the 23-year-old rookie.

"Jerry [Stackhouse] wanted him on his [practice] team early," Farrell noted. "He was a Bill Laimbeer-, Rick Mahorn-type, a hard-nosed kid who had been grounded in the fundamentals.

"He caught the eye of the veterans because of his hard work and dedication. He has a very good future in this league."

George Irvine, who coached the Pistons when Cardinal was a rookie, also believes Cardinal has a solid future in the league.

"He can last a long time," Irvine said. "He helps a team. I wish we could have played him more.

"Competitive guys help you win games, and that's what Brian is."

Joe Dumars, who played on the Pistons' championship squads of 1989 and 1990 and is now the team president for basketball operations, liked what Cardinal did as a rookie but wanted to see more productivity.

"What attracted us to Brian was the way he played the game. Last year [2000], he made the team on his sheer hustle, but I met with him after the season and told him to make it further, he'd have to work on his overall skill level," Dumars said. "This summer [2001], he was probably the best player on our [summer league] team. He developed range on his shot, and I'm pleased with his progress."

Cleaves, Atkins, and Moore were other Pistons who were members of the summer league team.

In the three-game summer league in Orlando for rookies, free agents, and others with limited NBA experience, Cardinal was the top scorer, averaging 16.3 points a game and making half of his three-point attempts.

"He's never going to be a star, but he's the kind of kid a team needs to have," Farrell said. "He's a great kid and one of the nice success stories in sports you like to see."

Former Detroit teammate Jud Buechler—who was traded to Phoenix during the off-season—said attitude is what sets Cardinal apart from many athletes.

"He gets there early and stays late," Buechler said. "Nowadays if you do that in the NBA, people want you around. He's thankful for being there and doesn't take it for granted.

"I don't necessarily see him being a starter, but I see a long NBA career for him. He provides energy and enthusiasm."

When Bruce Weber was an assistant at Purdue, he explained to Cardinal that unless a player is a bonafide superstar, they must willingly accept a lesser role to maintain longevity in the NBA.

"The thing I emphasized to Brian is that Stephen Scheffler [who played at Purdue from 1987 to 1990] could accept being a player on the bench and made the most out of it," Weber said.

"Maybe Brian can be a journeyman in the NBA."

Cardinal's collegiate nickname didn't follow him to the NBA, but he wasn't without one for long.

Jerome Williams, then a teammate with the Pistons, dubbed Cardinal "The Custodian" in October 2000.

"He was mopping up at both ends of the floor," Williams told reporters.

Williams had never seen Cardinal play until he arrived at the Pistons' training camp. He admits that his original impression wasn't favorable.

"When I first saw him, I said to myself, 'Why did the Pistons draft this guy?'" Williams said. "I was trying to picture in my mind what he could do.

"I said he might have a pretty good jump shot, but when he stepped on the floor and had those knee pads on, I said to myself, 'I can imagine he has more to offer than a jump shot.'

"When he started diving on the floor, I said he was mopping up the competition. His drive was carrying him to another level, and I admired him for that."

Williams believes Cardinal can stay in the NBA.

"He's got my three D's down—dedication, determination, and discipline," Williams said. "There's always a team that wants a team player."

If Cardinal's playing career doesn't work out, former high school teammate Eric Stevens can't see Cardinal far removed from basketball.

"Everyone is expecting him to be the next Gene Keady," Stevens said. "I think he'd make an excellent coach. He has taught me a lot about concentration and working toward a goal."

Former Unity assistant Gary Wilsey, named head coach at Mount Vernon (Indiana) High School prior to the 2001-02 school year, could see that happening.

"He'd make an excellent coach," Wilsey said. "He's the smartest basketball mind I've been around.

"He was in tune with everything you said. He's an excellent listener and absorbs things very well. You only had to tell him once."

Upcoming Cardinal family reunions are certain to find one issue that will be a topic for debate.

True, Brian Cardinal is the first family member to play basketball professionally, but who is the family's best player?

For those with a quick answer, consider Troy Cardinal's insight.

"He has only beaten me one-on-one once in his life," said Troy, older than Brian by two years. "It was the last time we played, and I was still in high school."

The game took place in Marshall, Minnesota. Troy recalled winning the first two games the brothers played to 21 that day. Those triumphs boosted his confidence.

"I said, 'Let's put some money on the line. Loser buys Dairy Queen,'" Troy Cardinal said. "That was the first time we did that.

"Sure enough, he beats me like 21-10 or 21-11."

Troy Cardinal called for a rematch, but it didn't happen.

"He said, 'Nope, I'm done,' and started walking off," Troy related.

Brian Cardinal received his treat that day. Troy has been left waiting to prove himself again.

"Honestly, I wouldn't mind [a rematch]," he said. "I'm up for the challenge."

When Troy Cardinal has a chance to watch the Pistons—and his little brother—on television, he has a different view than his friends.

"My friends treat him like I think of other NBA players—awe-struck," said Troy Cardinal, a technology consultant for an accounting firm.

He's not envious, however, of the most famous family member.

"I don't know fully what he has had to go through, but it's something I could never have brought myself through," Troy said.

"I have a lot of respect and admiration for him. We all have gifts, our own things we're supposed to do. Our job is to use those gifts. For me, I'm in the business of consulting. Brian has a different set of gifts."

In a phrase, he is able to have a ball playing a game.

(Photo Gold and Black Illustrated)

Brian Cardinal's
High School Statistics

YR	HT.	RECORD	FG-FGA	3P-3PA	FT-FTA	REB	AST	TP	AVG
91-92	6-3	10-14	47-101	0-0	18-35	46	10	112	5.9
92-93	6-5	22-6	198-333	1-5	86-119	257	53	483	17.2
93-94	6-7	27-1	155-305	53-110	130-177	228	76	493	23.5
94-95	6-8	27-4	246-461	67-171	165-264	325	95	724	24.1
Total		**86-25**	**646-1200**	**121-286**	**399-595**	**856**	**234**	**1,812**	**18.5**

Note: High-game scoring was 17 points in 1991-92; 34 points in 1992-93; 40 points in 1993-94 and 40 points in 1994-95.

Brian Cardinal's
High School Highlights

—Dec. 8, 1992: Sophomore Brian Cardinal rebounded a missed shot by his brother, Troy, and scored with four seconds to play. Thanks to his basket, Unity defeated St. Joseph-Ogden 55-53, giving the Rockets' seniors (including Troy) their first victory over the rival Spartans.

—Feb. 26, 1993: Brian scored 26 points and Troy had 12 as Unity topped St. Joseph-Ogden 74-50 in a Class A regional championship game.

A report on the game in the local weekly newspaper, *The County Star*, included this commentary by sports writer Tim Mitchell: "Both boys always seem to know what the other is doing. They mesh like veteran ballet partners."

—Jan. 11, 1994: Brian made 10 of 15 field goal attempts and scored 33 points as Unity defeated Westville 67-48. Four of his baskets were from three-point range.

—Jan. 21, 1994: Cardinal scored 40 points as Unity improved to 17-0 with a 95-56 triumph over Heritage.

After the game, veteran Heritage coach Lyle Loman told *Champaign-Urbana News-Gazette* sports writer Lou Engel, "Cardinal is the best player I've seen in this area since Rick Schmidt [a St. Joseph-Ogden graduate who went on to lead the University of Illinois in scoring in 1974 and 1975]."

—Feb. 1, 1994: Cardinal scored 12 of his team-high 16 points in the fourth quarter as Unity overcame a four-point deficit in the period to edge Catlin 56-53.

—Feb. 18, 1994: Cardinal scored 14 of his game-high 18 points in the fourth quarter as Unity rallied to beat Oakwood 63-55. Unity trailed by three points entering the fourth quarter.

—Dec. 2, 1994: Despite being double-teamed, Brian Cardinal recorded a triple-double as Unity topped Monticello 90-72. He had 28 points, 17 rebounds, and 14 assists for a school ranked seventh in the state in Class A.

—Dec. 16, 1994: Cardinal made 20 of 24 free throws and had 40 points and 18 rebounds as Unity outscored Bismarck-Henning 82-75. He scored the first 10 points of the fourth quarter as his team took a 60-59 lead after trailing 55-50. He had 23 points in the quarter.

—March 3, 1995: Cardinal scored 39 points in Unity's 71-64 sectional championship conquest of Arthur. He also had 18 rebounds as the Rockets advanced to the super-sectional (Sweet Sixteen) for the second time in school history.

—April 15, 1995: Cardinal was the most valuable player in the Coca-Cola All-American contest at Indianapolis' Market Square Arena. In 24 minutes, he had 24 points and 13 rebounds for the West, which won 137-120.

—July 1, 1995: Cardinal was the most valuable player for the South, a 108-78 winner over the North in the annual Illinois Basketball Coaches Association All-Star Game for graduated seniors in Peoria. In 17 minutes, he had 13 points, seven rebounds, and five blocked shots. In the first five minutes he played, Cardinal scored 10 points.

Brian Cardinal's College Statistics

YR.	HT.	RECORD	FG-FGA	3P-3PA	FT-FTA	REB	AST	TP	AVG
95-96	6-8	26-6	——Redshirted——						
96-97	6-8	18-12	100-220	21-63	98-139	182	58	319	10.6
97-98	6-8	28-8	140-275	30-70	122-155	178	66	432	12.0
98-99	6-8	23-13	118-246	37-99	114-147	186	82	387	11.4
99-00	6-8	24-10	137-333	42-124	130-169	203	71	446	13.9
Total		**119-49**	**495-1074**	**130-356**	**464-610**	**749**	**277**	**1584**	**12.0**

Note: High-game scoring was 25 points in 1996-97, 24 points in 1997-98, 33 points in 1998-99 and 29 points in 1999-2000.

Brian Cardinal's College Highlights

—Nov. 26, 1996: In his second collegiate game, Cardinal collected a double-double, with 13 points and 12 rebounds against Western Michigan, helping Purdue to a 65-56 victory.

—March 14, 1997: A redshirt freshman, Cardinal made a three-pointer with 16.7 seconds left to force overtime against Rhode Island in an NCAA Southeast Regional game at Memphis. Purdue went on to win 83-76.

—Nov. 29, 1997: A sophomore who was chosen as a team captain, Cardinal made 8 of 12 field goal attempts and scored 18 points against fourth-ranked North Carolina in a 73-69 loss.

—March 4, 1999: A junior who became an All-Big Ten third-team selection, he had a career-high 33 points (and made five of 10 three-point shots) in a 79-73 overtime Big Ten Conference Tournament loss to Michigan.

—March 14, 1999: He had a game-high 20 points as Purdue beat No. 2-seed Miami (Florida) in the second round of the NCAA East Regional at Boston.

—Jan. 12, 2000: Cardinal, an All-Big Ten second-team selection, had 21 points and 11 rebounds as Purdue upset No. 11 Indiana 83-77.

—March 23, 2000: Cardinal had 10 points, a game-high eight rebounds, and a team-high five assists in a 75-66 win over Gonzaga in the NCAA West Regional semifinals at Albuquerque, New Mexico.

—April 1, 2000: Cardinal scored three points at Indianapolis' Conseco Fieldhouse, but his NABC team came up short, 82-80. For the winning team, the Harlem Globetrotters, it was their 1,215th consecutive victory.

—Cardinal is the only athlete in Purdue history to win both the Mr. Hustle Award (for determination, drive, and leadership) and the Courage Award (for taking charges) four years in a row.

—Cardinal is one of only six players in 103 years of Purdue basketball to amass at least 1,000 points (he had 1,584), 500 rebounds (he had 749), and 200 assists (he had 277).

—Cardinal ranks first at the school and fourth among all players ever in the Big Ten Conference for steals in a career (259) and, as a rookie, broke Purdue's 21-year-old record for steals in a season by a freshman (held by Kyle Macy in 1975-76) with 51.

Brian Cardinal's
Professional Statistics

YR.	HT.	RECORD	FG-FGA	3P-3PA	FT-FTA	REB	AST	TP	AVG
00-01	6-8	32-50	10-31	0-5	11-18	23	3	31	2.1

Note: High-game scoring was nine points.

Brian Cardinal's Professional Highlights

—June 28, 2000: A second-round draft selection by the Detroit Pistons, the 44th player picked overall.

—Oct. 10, 2000: Scored eight points and had four rebounds in eight minutes in team's exhibition opener, a 101-97 victory vs. Cleveland.

—Oct. 14, 2000: Scored eight points in 11 minutes against Orlando. Detroit lost the exhibition game 118-92.

—Dec. 9, 2000: Scored three points in 15 minutes in his regular-season debut against Portland. Detroit lost 114-83.

—April 12, 2001: Scored a season-high nine points against Toronto. He helped the Pistons overcome a 17-point second-half deficit (58-41) to win 99-87 and was named Player of the Game. Detroit went on a 35-7 second-half run, fueled by eight points and four defensive rebounds by Cardinal during a seven-minute stretch.

—April 17, 2001: Scored seven points in a season-high 21 minutes at Toronto. The Raptors won in overtime 94-92 before a crowd of 19,800.

About the Author . . .

Fred Kroner has been a member of the sports staff at the *Champaign-Urbana (Illinois) News-Gazette* since 1981 and has written for daily newspapers since 1975. He covers high school and collegiate sports.

A newspaper series he authored in 1985 on drug and alcohol use and abuse by high school athletes was nominated for a Pulitzer Prize. Kroner was the recipient of Associated Press writing awards in 1978, 1985, and 1989, and three times has been named Newsman of the Year by the Illinois Wrestling Coaches and Officials Association (1984, 1988, and 2000).

In July 2001, he was one of three journalists from Illinois to participate in the Second Annual Sports Media Practitioner Workshop in Antigua.

The 45-year-old Kroner was a contributing author to several poetry anthologies, including *A Cascade of Memories* in 1998 and *Enlightened Shadows* in 2001.

He was listed in Marquis' millennium edition of *Who's Who in America* in 2000 as well as in Strathmore's *Who's Who Millennium Edition* in 2001.

Kroner is a 1978 graduate of the University of Illinois and a 1973 graduate of Mahomet-Seymour (Illinois) High School.

He has one son, Devin Kroner, and three stepchildren, Salim Belahi, Jamel Belahi, and Malika Belahi. In 1999, he married the woman he has adored since high school, Emily Moon.

Fred Kroner

His hobbies include traveling, writing poetry, and gardening.